# HAPPY BIRTHDAY

Ellyn Sanna

HUMBLECREEK
INSPIRATION FOR LIFE

*This* is your day, the special day
when you entered the world, and on your birthday,
I want to take this chance to tell you
how I feel about you all year round.
You are a gift from God to everyone who knows you,
and today and always, my heart brims with wishes
and prayers for the life that lies ahead of you.

# Contents

1. I'm Glad God Made You . . . . . . . . . . . . . . . . . . . . 7
2. Birthday Milestones . . . . . . . . . . . . . . . . . . . . . . 17
3. Wishing You Joy . . . . . . . . . . . . . . . . . . . . . . . . . . 25
4. Wishing You Peace . . . . . . . . . . . . . . . . . . . . . . . 29
5. Wishing You Love . . . . . . . . . . . . . . . . . . . . . . . . 33
6. Birthday Prayers . . . . . . . . . . . . . . . . . . . . . . . . . 37

Happy birthday to you!

Happy birthday to you!

Happy birthday, oh dear one,

Happy birthday to you!

# Celebration

## 1

## I'm Glad God Made You

God is still creating the world, you know, adding details, perfecting, creating entire new things that no one has ever seen before. And we are each part of His creation. Nor are our births the end of the story—look into your own heart and you will see all the amazing things He is creating, if you will only let Him. And I, for one, am glad, glad, glad—not only that God made you, but that He continues to make you, year after year.

LUCIE CHRISTOPHER

If I had a single flower
for every time I think about you,
I could walk forever in my garden.

CLAUDIA GRANDI

. . .

*My thoughts are full of you today—*

*and each new thought makes me smile.*

. . . .

I thank my God upon every remembrance of you.

PHILIPPIANS 1:3

# A Heavenly Celebration

There's a birthday song for children that goes something like this: "On the day you were born, an angel shouted and blew on his horn." I can just imagine the scene in heaven, everyone shouting and clapping, a riot of music filling the heavenly vault, smiles of joy on each celestial face—all because your mother had just given birth to you!

The angels still celebrate your birth. So do I—and so does God.

# Unique and Special

God's creation is lavish—such detailed beauty, so many creatures, such lovely abundance. His delight in His creation never tires, as moment by moment He continues to design snowflakes and DNA cells, supernova and galaxies, no two alike, each one unique and special.

You, too, are a part of God's creation, a special and essential part of His plan for our world. No one else can take your place. No one else can be you.

I'm so glad God created you!

. . . .

You are a part of the great plan, an indispensable part.
You are needed; you have your own unique share
in the freedom of Creation.

MADELEINE L'ENGLE

And God saw every thing

that he had made, and,

behold, it was very good.

GENESIS 1:31

• • •

Think of it—not one whorled finger exactly like another!
If God should take such delight in designing fingertips,
think how much pleasure the unfurling
of your life must give Him.

LUCIE CHRISTOPHER

# Celebrate!

Creation would have been incomplete without you.
God knew how much the world needed your smile,
Your hands,
Your voice,
Your way of thinking,
Your insights,
Your love.
God speaks through you in a way He can through no other.
Be true to the person He created.
Celebrate the birthday gift of your self.

GWYNETH GAVIN

# Birthdays and Flowers

One way to celebrate your own special day is with these jewels and flowers that honor each month:

- JANUARY: garnet and carnation

- FEBRUARY: amethyst and violet

- MARCH: aquamarine and jonquil

- APRIL: diamond and sweet pea

- MAY: emerald and lily of the valley

- JUNE: pearl and rose

- JULY: ruby and larkspur

- AUGUST: peridot and gladiolus

- SEPTEMBER: sapphire and aster

- OCTOBER: opal and calendula

- NOVEMBER: topaz and chrysanthemum

- DECEMBER: turquoise and narcissus

- - -

*Flowers preach to us if we will hear.*

CHRISTINA ROSSETTI

What would I have done if God hadn't made you?
The world wouldn't have been the same.
All the talks that we've had, all the laughter we've shared,
Could not be replaced, by fortune nor fancy nor fame.

ALEXANDRA ELIZONDO

. . .

My heart is full of gratitude,
today and always,
for all that you mean to me!

# One Thing I'd Give

My friend,
If I could give you one thing,
I would wish for you the ability
To see yourself as others see you.
Then you would realize
What a truly
Special person you are.

B. A. BILLINGSLY

# Celebration

## 2

## Birthday Milestones

There is something satisfying, rejuvenating, comforting about the seasons. . . . The seasons remind me that I play one small part in a bigger picture—that there is a pulse, a sequence, a journey set into motion by the very hand of God Himself.

KAREN SCALF LINAMEN

# Time's Gifts

Why is it that children celebrate each birthday milestone with joy and triumph—but adults go into either real or mock mourning as each milestone is achieved? The reason has to do, I think, with our culture's attitude about growing older: Up to about age twenty-five, the added years are welcomed—but for the remaining fifty or sixty years of our lives, we act as though the passage of time were a sad secret, a source of shame and regret.

How silly! Celebrate your years. Be grateful for all the gifts time has given you. God has meaning and purpose for each season of your life—and with each birthday milestone, you can celebrate all He's taught you. After all, in Christ, little by little, year by year, God transforms you into His image.

Let time flow by,
with which we flow on to be transformed
into the glory of the children of God.

FRANCIS DE SALES

• • •

Time is the herald of Truth.

ELIZABETH GRYMESTON

• • •

...As if you could kill time without injuring eternity.

HENRY DAVID THOREAU

19

# Bloom and Be Fruitful

Our culture's emphasis on youth is skewed. Why did we ever get the idea that our worth diminishes with the passing years? After all, look at the natural world. The mature plants, not the immature, are the ones that flower and yield fruit.

With each passing year, may you see your life bursting into fresh bloom, yielding a richer and richer harvest of the Spirit's fruit.

· · · ·

The fruit of the Spirit is love, joy, peace, longsuffering,
gentleness, goodness, faith, meekness, temperance.

GALATIANS 5:22–23

I am the vine, ye are the branches:
He that abideth in me, and I in him,
the same bringeth forth much fruit.

JOHN 15:5

. . .

*I have chosen you, and ordained*

*you, that ye should go and*

*bring forth fruit, and that*

*your fruit should remain.*

JOHN 15:16

. . .

Be patient therefore. . . . Behold, the husbandman waiteth for
the precious fruit of the earth, and hath long patience for it,
until he receive the early and latter rain. Be ye also patient. . . .

JAMES 5:7–8

## The Precious Things in Life

Time is wonderful gift given to us by God—so don't fear the passing years. Celebrate them! The best things in life, the truly precious things, get better with time; each year only increases their value.

Your life is like that, too. For each year that I know you, I appreciate you more and more. I'm so thankful for your life.

The here-and-now is no mere filling of time,
but a filling of time with God.

JOHN FOSTER

• • •

Time wasted is existence;

time used is life.

EDWARD YOUNG

• • •

Make use of time, let not advantage slip;
Beauty within itself should not be wasted.

WILLIAM SHAKESPEARE

## My Wish for You

On your birthday, as you look at your life, may you rejoice in all the years have brought you—and may you recognize the fruit of the Spirit ripening year by year. I especially wish you the bright, sweet fruits of joy and peace and love.

# Celebration

## 3
### Wishing You Joy

Enter thou into the joy of thy lord.

MATTHEW 25:21

# A Gift from God

With time, we often lose a child's knack for simply being happy. We have so many serious responsibilities that we almost feel guilty if we feel joyful, as though we don't deserve to be so happy.

But joy is one of God's gifts, the fruit of the Spirit at work in your life. So on this special day—and all year long—rejoice! Be glad! Celebrate!

· · ·

*With. . .the deep power of joy,*

*we see into the life of things.*

WILLIAM WORDSWORTH

How fit to employ
All the heart and the soul and the senses forever in joy!

ROBERT BROWNING

. . .

*Ask, and ye shall receive,*

*that your joy may be full.*

JOHN 16:24

. . .

This is the true joy in life,
the being used for a purpose recognized by
yourself as a mighty one.

GEORGE BERNARD SHAW

Let all thy joys be as the month of May,
And all thy days be as a marriage day:
Let sorrow, sickness, and a troubled mind
Be stranger to thee.

FRANCIS QUARLES

. . .

*Happiness is not a possession to be prized,*

*it is a quality of thought,*

*a state of mind.*

DAPHNE DU MAURIER

. . .

Happiness is as a butterfly, which, when pursued, is always
beyond our grasp, but which, if you will sit down quietly,
may alight upon you.

NATHANIEL HAWTHORNE

# Celebration

## 4

## Wishing You Peace

Peace be within thy walls,
and prosperity within thy palaces.

PSALM 122:7

# Undisturbed Peace

Life is so busy, so hectic and rushed. Take time this year to slow down, to make space in your life for peace. And even on the busiest, most frantic days this year holds for you, my prayer is this: May the Holy Spirit's peace dwell undisturbed within your heart.

• • •

Peace I leave with you,
my peace I give unto you:
not as the world giveth,
give I unto you.
Let not your heart be troubled,
neither let it be afraid.

JOHN 14:27

And the peace of God, which passeth all understanding,
shall keep your hearts and minds through Christ Jesus.

PHILIPPIANS 4:7

• • •

And in *His* will is our peace.

DANTE

• • •

. . .there is a country
Far beyond the stars
Where stands a winged sentry
All skillful in the wars:
There, above noise and danger,
Sweet Peace is crown'd with smiles,
And One born in a manger
Commands the beauteous files.

HENRY VAUGHAN

Over all the mountaintops is peace.
In all treetops you perceive scarcely a breath.
The little birds in the forest are silent.
Wait then; soon you, too, will have peace.

JOHANN WOLFGANG VON GOETHE

. . .

*P*eace is not something you wish for;
it's something you make, something you do,
something you are, and something you give away.

ROBERT FULGHUM

. . .

Do not let trifles disturb your tranquility of mind. . . .
Life is too precious to be sacrificed for
the nonessential and transient. . . .
Ignore the inconsequential.

GRENVILLE KLEISER

# Celebration

## 5

## Wishing You Love

Love is of God;
and every one that loveth is born of God,
and knoweth God.

1 JOHN 4:7

# True Love

When I say I wish you love today, that's just another way of saying that on your birthday, and always, I wish for God's presence in your life. I hope you know how much you are loved. And may love continue to spill out of you to the world around you, for God is always present wherever true love lives.

One word
frees us of all the weight and pain of life:
That word is love.
SOPHOCLES

I live and love in God's peculiar light.
MICHELANGELO

All love is sweet,
Given or returned. Common as light is love,
And its familiar voice wearies not ever. . . .

PERCY BYSSHE SHELLEY

. . .

*Love comforteth like*

*sunshine after rain.*

WILLIAM SHAKESPEARE

. . .

Thou shalt love and be loved by, forever:
a Hand like this hand
Shall throw open the gates of new life to thee!
See the Christ. . . !

ROBERT BROWNING

Nothing is sweeter than love, nothing higher, nothing broader, nothing better, either in Heaven or earth; because love is born of God, and, rising above all created things can find rest in Him alone.

THOMAS À KEMPIS

. . .

*Y*ou will find as you look back upon your life that the moments when you have really lived are the moments when you have done things in the spirit of love.

HENRY DRUMMOND

. . .

Though I speak with the tongues of men and of angels, and have not charity [love], I am become as sounding brass, or a tinkling cymbal. And though I have the gift of prophecy, and understand all mysteries, and all knowledge; and though I have all faith, so that I could remove mountains, and have not charity, I am nothing.

1 CORINTHIANS 13:1–2

# Celebration

## 6

## Birthday Prayers

God grant you many and happy years,
Till, when the last has crowned you,
The dawn of endless days appears,
And heaven is shining around you.

OLIVER WENDELL HOLMES

# Birthday Traditions

* The cake is one of our most common birthday traditions. The lit candles stand for the achievement of each year of the past, while the blown out candles symbolize our hopes for the future.

*I pray that your birthday will be lit with the sweet recognition of each year—and that God will grant you your heart's desires for the future.*

* Some families have the birthday person wear a "jeweled" crown for the celebration, making that person king or queen for the day.

*I pray that you will recognize the royal heritage you have in Christ.*

* Other families have a special red plate that the birthday person uses for their meals. This tradition is said to date back to the early Americans, who used the red plate as a visual reminder of the love and esteem in which they held the birthday person.

*I pray that your day will be filled with reminders of love.*

* In my family, as a child my favorite birthday tradition was that the birthday person was freed for the day from even the simplest chores. This family custom told the birthday person: "You are loved. You are special. Enjoy your day!"

*I pray that on your birthday you will take time to relax and enjoy the things that please you most.*

On your birthday and always, I pray these things. . .

*May you celebrate your life. You are wonderful, one-of-a-kind, and so very special. Only you can be you; no one else can do that job. So I pray that you will spread God's light with all the unique gifts He created in you.*

*May you celebrate the passing years. Each one adds wisdom and experience, insight and new skills. Take joy in time's gifts, and do not fear the future. Each new year holds new blessings. I pray you will see the Spirit's fruit grow riper with each year.*

*May you celebrate all that God is doing in your life. This year, open your heart to God. Dance with joy, rest in peace, live in love. I pray that you will know the full goodness of life.*

*Happy Birthday!*